First Edition

Printed in the U.S.A.

DEDICATION

This book is dedicated to:

My daughters Lucia, Emily and Sofia who are my motivation in

Life and the inspiration to continue pursuing my dreams, and

for everyone who is willing to save our planet.

INTRODUCTION

"The Quest for Saving the Environment" is the story of a little girl named Lucia that is determined along with her friends to make sure people are more aware of the environment in order to save the planet from pollution.

The book is designed for young children to learn in a fun and interesting way the power of the three R's *"Reduce, Reuse and Recycle"*. It also brings opportunity for children to enrich their knowledge in math, science and social studies with examples and activities that make this book very attractive.

Join Lucia and her friends in this adventure where everything could be possible if we have the determination. Let's save our home " The Planet Earth".

Once upon a time there was a little girl named Lucia who lived with her mom, dad and her sisters Emily and Sofia. Lucia is a very friendly girl who loves to explore her environment. Her favorite thing to do besides playing outside and playing with her sisters is to do science experiments.

Lucia and Emily do many things together. They go outside to bike, they go to the park and also they do crafts. On summer time, they go to the pool and visit her relatives. One morning Lucia was having an issue about sharing. "That is my water bottle", said Lucia. But " I want it", Emily cried.

Why do not you share with your sister one of your water bottles since you have another one?, asked mom. Ok mom, but please Emily be nice with it. Lucia said. Did you know that you could be helping our planet by doing that? said father. Really dad?, Lucia was surprised for her dad's question.

Of course, you would be reducing and reusing. What do you mean dad? Asked Lucia. Well said father, you would be reducing by sharing it, and you will be reusing by letting Emily to use it. That is very interesting…

Lucia just learned something interesting that morning thanks to her little sister and her water bottle.

When Lucia was at school, she was still thinking that somehow she helped the environment that morning. She mentioned it to her teacher. Then the teacher said "Lucia you were really helping the environment". Children let's read a book about it", said the teacher.

Is the Earth really our home? asked Lucia. Yes! And that is why we have to protect the environment, said the teacher. Pollution is a big problem for the environment the teacher kept saying. "What is pollution?" Lucia asked. Well said the teacher, Pollution is when the environment is not clean and the planet gets sick"…

… But the teacher said to the children that they can save the planet with the Power of the three R's:

Reduce, Reuse and Recycle.

Reduce: to make something smaller or use less.

Reuse : You can "reuse" materials in their original form instead of throwing.

Recycle: don't just toss everything in the trash.

Because the children were so interested in learning about how to protect the environment, the teacher gave them a special assignment:

"Children how could you apply the power of the three R's at home?".

At dismiss time, Lucia and her cousin Guido were talking about school… I am very excited about this assignment. I think this will be the first time I will do something to help the environment. What about you? Asked Lucia …

I think that will be my first time too… answered Guido.

When Lucia got home from school she started to talk about the environment … Mom, I learned interesting facts today at school about pollution and the power of the three R's.

That is wonderful Lucia! – exclaimed her mom. Helping and protecting the environment is part of our duty. I am glad that you learned about it .

Pollution means any contamination of air, soil, water and environment. Noise and sound are also a part of pollution.

Lucia decided to start working on her assignment. Emily wanted to help so she asked Lucia - Can I please help you? Sure, let me show you the book I got from school about the environment. Lucia and Emily spent quite time together learning about how pollution makes the earth sick and how the power of the three R's can help to reduce that problem.

Emily proudly said: " the power of the three R's are Reduce,

Reuse and Recycle". I think we can work with them…

THE POWER OF THE THREE R'S

REDUCING :

From now on Lucia helped her mom to remind her to always bring reusable bags to the supermarket and to refuse to get plastic bags from the store.

THE POWER OF THE THREE R'S

REUSING :

Lucia though that a good way to reuse was sharing with her sister Emily the clothes that did not fit her anymore and the toys that she did not play with them anymore.

Lucia's generosity made Emily very happy. And the good example made her do the same thing. She gave her old bicycle to her little sister Sofia.

Reusing is a great thing to do and it can make people happy. What do you think?...

THE POWER OF THE THREE R'S

RECYCLING :

Lucia was thrilled to protect the environment. She collected and classified plastic bottles, plastic bags, aluminum cans, newspapers and cardboards in order to put them in the recycle bin where they belong.

Back at school, Lucia and her classmates shared their assignments and the teacher was happy to announced that it was a success thanks to the correct use of the three R's!. Let's sing a song:

The Power of the three R's

The Power of the three R's

are easy to apply

Once you start to use them all the time.

Wonderful things

you will be doing

By Reducing, Reusing

and Recycling your trash.

QUEST FOR SAVING THE ENVIRONMENT'S IDEAS:

At home: We can help our parents to **recycle**, classify and organize the trash before putting them in the recycle bin where they belong. You can also keep track on how much trash you make at home.

- You can **reuse** by donating to Goodwill or Salvation Army stuff that are still in good shape but you do not use them anymore.

- You can **reduce** but using less paper at home or school and you will be saving trees!

Recycling Word Search

```
R R E C Y C L E V B I L M O
E G P O U I R S L W I U F B
P P N E N V I R O N M E N T
A L U I Q E K L E E B W R W
P A I B G A S C R O T E K N
S S Z C S A U U T F P S D E
W T A W Y D K T E A W Q A E
E I S T E X L C P R B J E W
N C R R S E U V A E G H C C
K G F Y S O C G N P Z L N X
```

BOTTLES   ENVIRONMENT   NEWSPAPER

PACKAGING   PAPER   PLASTIC

RECYCLE   REDUCE   REUSE

DID YOU KNOW?

RECYCLE Symbol History:

The COLOR that most often symbolizes recycling is **Green**. However, there are many Graphic SYMBOLS for RECYCLING: Scroll down and see what you find!

The recycling symbol you see today with three arrows in the triangle shape was designed in 1970 as part of a contest sponsored by the Container Corporation of America (CCA) (now Jefferson Smurfit Corporation). As a special event for the original Earth Day in 1970 (started by John Mc Connell), CCA conducted a contest for graphic art students to design a symbol representing paper recycling. The winning entry was submitted by Gary Dean Anderson, a 5-year architecture student at the University of Southern California at Los Angels. Later that year, William Lloyd, modified the contest winning recycling symbol to create the present-day image

This collection is the best web-wide:

Recycle Symbols of the world, glass, plastic, paper, wood, metal, cardboard, batteries, soil, packaging symbols, globes and recycle clip art.

Reflection

The book was quite a good experience for myself as a future educator and as a human being. Awareness of the protection of the environment is a fact that we all should apply in our daily basics.

Children are the most motivated people who are eager to apply their knowledge in the real world and we have to take advantage of that by teaching them to love their home " Earth" and its environment.

My children who I dedicated this book and the ones that I read the book not only liked the message, they also understood the importance of being aware of the environment. Their reactions were positive and now they will try to be more careful before they put the trash away. Another good reaction was that one of them told me that reusing and reducing can help the environment and also can help our economy. That was good thinking because the more we spend the more trash we create.

This book also benefited my children from what the real purpose of this book was, integrate social studies, math and science concepts in a simple, interesting and fun way!

Citations

1. http:// www.socialstudies.org/standards/teacherstandards

The mission of National Council for the Social Studies is to provide leadership, service, and support for all social studies educators.

2. http://kids.niehs.nih.gov/explore/reduce/

The National Institute of Environmental Health Sciences, created a friendly website for children where they can get information related to the environment, including fun science activities and games.

3. http://www.planetpals.com/recycle-symbol-history.html

Planetpals embrace today's world by covering topics that affect kids on a social and environmental level. Planetpals is a unique property that engages kids to think about their world, their health and relationships with slogans such as "Be Healthy Inside And Out".

The End